SPUR PUBLICATIONS

SIR WALTER GILBEY SERIES

CONCISE HISTORY OF
THE SHIRE HORSE

ORIGINALLY PUBLISHED AS
THE GREAT HORSE
OR SHIRE HORSE

Engraved by J. B. Pratt

ARMOUR CLAD GERMAN KNIGHT OF THE 15TH OR 16TH CENTURY
after a Painting by Hans Burgkmair

OTHER BOOKS AVAILABLE

Concise History of the Shire Horse

Originally published as
The Great Horse or Shire Horse

by
SIR WALTER GILBEY, BART

SECOND EDITION RE-ISSUED

PUBLISHED BY THE SPUR PUBLICATIONS COMPANY

Hill Brow, Liss, Hampshire, GU33 7PU

© The Spur Publications Company 1976

ISBN 0 904558 13 4

First edition 1889 as: "THE
GREAT HORSE OR THE
WAR HORSE: from the time of
the Roman Invasion till its
development into the SHIRE
HORSE".

Printed and bound in Great Britain by
Redwood Burn Limited, Trowbridge & Esher
for the publishers
THE SPUR PUBLICATIONS COMPANY
Hill Brow, Liss, Hampshire, GU33 7PU

PREFACE TO THE SECOND EDITION.

SINCE the publication in 1889 of the first edition of this little book, which I was privileged to dedicate to His Royal Highness the Duke of Cambridge, great progress has been made in the improvement of the Shire Horse. It therefore has seemed desirable to remodel and enlarge, by the inclusion of more minute details, pages which had been compiled from notes taken in course of an enquiry into the antecedents of the horse now known as the Shire-bred. This research led to the conclusion that the Shire Horse is the purest survival of the type described by mediæval writers as the Great Horse; and this type being the native development of that ancient British War Horse which evoked the admiration of Julius Cæsar, it seemed appropriate to seek permission to dedicate the book to the Prince who combined with his high position as Commander-in-Chief of Her Majesty's Forces, the keenest interest in those breeds of horses which are most useful to the State.

It would be easy to multiply *ad infinitum* such evidence as is here quoted, but it is unnecessary to encumber the narrative with repetition of details which throw no fresh light upon the history of the breed. These pages have been written for the convenience of those who desire to possess in concise form knowledge of the main facts concerning the origin and development of this truly noble and most useful animal, and to point out the true type of the " Shire Horse." It is not claimed that there is any information contained in this work which those who are interested in the subject may not, with an equal amount of patient reading obtain for themselves.

Elsenham Hall, Essex,

CONTENTS.

———

ILLUSTRATIONS.

A HISTORY TRACING

THE SHIRE HORSE

TO THE

OLD ENGLISH GREAT HORSE

(THE WAR HORSE).

———◆———

INTRODUCTION.

THE number of books about horses which
have been printed is very large; a good
authority states that the total is upward of
four thousand volumes; and therefore another
seems almost superfluous. Yet from that
early book of Wynkyn de Worde, printed
in A.D. 1500, Thomas Blundeville's in 1566,
the Duke of Newcastle's in 1658, and the
work by Sir Wm. Hope, Kt., Deputy
Lieutenant of Edinburgh Castle, published in
1717, to the host of books on horses which
have appeared during the last twenty years,
there is not one which can be said to render
full justice to the peculiarly English breed
whose history it is proposed to examine.

By the exercise of care and judgment

1

Englishmen have achieved many triumphs as breeders of domestic animals; and none of these, perhaps, are more conspicuous than the establishment of the two types of horse —the race horse and heavy draught horse; breeds differing as widely one from the other as the greyhound differs from the mastiff. Each horse is in its own way almost perfect; the former having been brought to the highest state of development for speed, the latter to the highest development of strength; and it would be difficult to maintain that one is more beautiful than the other. Many volumes have been written on the racehorse, and innumerable lives and fortunes have been devoted to perfecting the breed; and if little has been written concerning the draught horse, it will be possible to show that for generations before our time no little attention has been bestowed also upon his improvement.

The aim of the following pages is to set out in convenient form some facts relating to the heavy horse as it existed during the early and middle ages, long before it was brought into general use for farm work and for drawing heavy loads. Exceptional historic interest attaches to this breed; for its lot has been closely interwoven with that

of the people of Britain from the earliest
times. It is not a little curious to reflect
that the animal which formed the very
backbone of our ancestors' independence—
on which our forefathers depended for their
strength and prowess in the Art of War,
is the animal on which we depend to
carry on the operations of Agriculture and
Commerce—the arts of peace. It must not
be forgotten that the use of the horse in
agriculture is comparatively modern. In
England until the middle ages the work of
the farm and almost all heavy draught work
was performed by oxen. These animals
were in common use for farm work until the
latter half of the last century. Arthur
Young in his *General View of the Agriculture of Lincolnshire*, written in 1799,
mentions a farm he visited where he saw
"two (oxen) and a horse draw home in a
waggon as good loads of corn as are common in Suffolk with three horses." He says
further, " about Grantham many oxen have
been worked, but all have left off ; once they
were seen all the way from Grantham to
Lincoln, now scarcely any ; a pair of mares
and one man will do as much work as four
oxen and two men. . . . On the Wolds
most farmers have some oxen for working,

leading manure, corn and hay." When horses began to be employed by ordinary occupiers of land they were animals by no means remarkable for strength and substance ; "stots" and "affers," as these were called, were of a stamp distinct from the "Strong" or "Great" horses which in those days were bred and reserved for purposes neither agricultural nor commercial.

The early foundation stock from which investigation proves that our modern Shire horses are descended was brought to a high state of perfection for its special purpose, not only by the judicious introduction of foreign blood, but by wise enactments of the Legislature. We find in the old Statute Books numerous Acts of Parliament which supported private skill and enterprise in the endeavour to improve an animal on which, it may fairly be said, the safety of the nation in no small measure depended.

The facts which it is proposed to set before the reader are, for the most part, the fruit of careful research among old records ; and it must be added that figures worked in tapestry, rude paintings of incidents and illustrations which sometimes occur in these records, have frequently been more helpful than the manuscripts themselves. The artist perpetuates what the writer from sheer familiarity ignores ; and for this reason the works of old painters have been laid under contribution in the present survey of the Great Horse breed.

THE CHARIOT HORSE OF THE ANCIENT BRITONS.

No very profound enquiry is needed to furnish us with a starting point in the history of the Great Horse. We need go no farther than our old school friend Cæsar, and examine his account of the forces which resisted his descent upon England in the year 55 B.C.—nearly two thousand years ago. The following familiar passage (from Camden's translation, *Britannia*, 4th edition) throws valuable light on the stamp of horse which was employed in warfare by the early Britons :—

" Most of them use chariots in battle. They first scour up and down on every side, throwing their darts ; creating disorder among the ranks by the terror of their horses and noise of their chariot wheels. When they have got among the troops of [their enemies'] horse, they leap out of the chariots and fight on foot. Meantime the charioteers retire to a little distance from the field, and place themselves in such a manner that if the others be overpowered by the number of the enemy, they may be secure to make

good their retreat. Thus they act with the agility of
cavalry; and the steadiness of infantry in battle.
They become so expert by constant practice that in
declivities and precipices they can stop their horses
at full speed; and, on a sudden, check and turn them.
They run along the pole, stand on the yoke, and then,
as quickly, into their chariots again. They frequently
retreat on purpose, and after they have drawn men
from the main body, leap from their pole, and wage
an unequal war on foot."

It is obvious from this that the horses
used must have possessed strength, substance, courage and docility. The war
chariot of our forefathers was not a model
of elegance and lightness; it was required
to manœuvre over the roughest of ground,
carrying several fighting men, and the needful
strength could only be obtained as the result
of weight and clumsiness. To draw such a
vehicle at speed and force a way among
disciplined cavalry, horses of substance,
power, and courage were required; while
the ability of the charioteers to "stop their
horses at full speed; and on a sudden, check
and turn them," points not only to strength
and weight, but to docility and handiness.
Those who saw these animals have recorded
their admiration, holding them different from,
and superior to, any horses they had seen
before; and these witnesses, we must re-
member, were acquainted with most breeds

BRITISH COINS OF THE FIRST CENTURY.

of horses employed by the nations of
their time.

THE GREAT HORSE IN THE FIRST CENTURY.

Our next piece of evidence comes, not
from the writer but from the artist, if he
may be called so ; not from without the
shores of Britain but from within. For
some historical purposes coins serve a purpose as valuable as pictures, and the present
is a case in point. The coins of which
illustrations are here given are among the
very earliest known to have been struck
in this island. They date from the age
of Cunobelin (the First century), and are
therefore the production of a period when
neither Art nor Agriculture had place in
the country ; they are relics of a time when
the conditions of life required only the
herdsman and the soldier. With these facts
in mind we may examine these coins and
see what we can gather from them. The
fact that the device on each is a horse
suggests at once that this animal played a
most important part in the social economy
of the people who struck the coins. They
were among those found on the borders
of Norfolk, Suffolk and Cambridgeshire,

and are believed to have been circulated in the interest of the Iceni, a tribe which distinguished itself above all others by its resolute resistance to the Roman troops.

The head and front of the power of resistance displayed by the Iceni lay in their skilful employment of the war-chariot as a means of attack—in other words, in the efficiency of their powerful and disciplined horses. There was no agriculture among these people, and the importance of the horse which led to the adoption of its figure as a numismatic device was due to the part it played in war. Now these quaintly archaic designs must not be compared with the works of art by which Greek and Roman civilisation was made famous, and laughed aside as contemptible. The true standard of comparison is found in the rude figures in rock inscriptions, and in the ornamentation on the weapons and tools of what we now call savage races. Measured by this standard these designs boast merit, for the artist has succeeded in conveying an impression of the character of his ideal horse. His ideal was clearly one of deep-carcased, wide-buttocked breed, with profuse mane and tail ; a horse, in fact, which possessed some of the prominent

characteristics of the modern Shire horse.
Thus we have pictorial evidence to confirm
the written testimony of Julius Cæsar, that
twenty centuries ago there existed in Britain
a breed of horses having cardinal points in
common with those massive animals seen
to-day, known as Shires, Clydesdales and
Suffolks, and held in the highest esteem.

Parenthetically, it is worth noticing that
while a large proportion of the few coins
known to be British bear the effigy of a
horse, not one of the Roman coins figured
in Camden's *Britannia* bear such a device;
nor do the coins of Saxon origin. To a
horse-loving people this proof of the esteem
in which their forefathers held the animal is
particularly interesting. A large white horse
is stated by Mr. Walker, Camden's colla-
borator, to have been the ensign of Hengist
and Horsa, who landed in Britain in A.D.
449, and this seems to be the only instance
in which the figure of a horse was employed
as an emblem by others than the Britons.

Mr. Walker, whom Camden introduces as
the great expert of the day, remarks, *apropos*
of the coins figured in the *Britannia*, that
in ancient times special value attached to
white horses; in this respect, however,
horses were not singular, white animals of

all domesticated species being regarded with peculiar favour, and commonly selected as gifts to Royalty, and as ceremonial tribute when state or tribe was required to acknowledge suzerainty. Mr. Walker asserts also, that only men of the highest rank were permitted to ride white horses on state occasions. That the use of a white steed implied dignity is well shown by the treatment accorded John of France by Edward the Black Prince when he conducted the French King to London. Anxious that the captive should appear not as a prisoner but as a royal guest, John "was clad in royal robes, and was mounted on a white steed, distinguished by its beauty and size ; whilst the conqueror, in meaner attire, was carried by his side on a black palfrey." Richard Berenger, gentleman of the horse to George III., who wrote *The History and Art of Horsemanship*, published 1771, observes that "The King of Naples at this day pays an annual fief of a white horse to the See of Rome as acknowledgment for the kingdom which he holds from the Pope." Thus we see that the ceremonial value of the white horse was both ancient and lasting. We must not, however, allow this point to detain us.

FROM THE SEVENTH CENTURY TO THE CONQUEST.

The Venerable Bede says that the English did not commonly use saddle horses until about A.D. 631. At this period, which marks the dawn of the Christian era in Britain, preaching monks travelled the country, and it was considered a mark of humility for these early missionaries to travel on foot. Prelates and churchmen of rank were allowed by law to ride, but were counselled to use mares, in order to spare the horses for military purposes. It is to be observed that, although cavalry as a fighting arm was unknown in Britain for the first thousand years of the Christian era, horses of a sturdy and enduring stamp were as essential to the efficiency of troops, as they became at a later date when armoured horsemen formed perhaps the most formidable part of an army. Until they acquired the knowledge from their Norman conquerors, the inhabitants of this country knew nothing of the art of fighting on horseback, but at the same time the " theigns and hus-carles "—picked household troops, generally consisting of big men—employed horses to carry them from place to place, and as these wore chain mail, and had to accomplish long arduous marches over road-less country, a big and powerful stamp of horse was just as necessary to them as it would have been had actual fighting in the saddle been the profession of the riders.

It is conjectured that this early "mounted infantry" system was copied from the Danes, who used horses, acquired locally, in this fashion when they made their descents upon the east coast of England ; this, how-ever by the way. The first mention in history of a Master of the Horse occurs in King Alfred's reign (871-901.) His *Hors-Theign* was named Ecquef. The bare fact that such an office existed is worth mention, as showing the existence of a royal stud in those days. Richard Berenger gives parti-culars of the curious and interesting laws framed in the tenth century by Howel Dda, the "Good" Welsh Prince. Space considerations forbid their inclusion here ; it must suffice to say that these laws prove how great was the importance attached to possession of horses. The first piece of legislation that points to foreign apprecia-tion of English-bred horses occurs in the reign of Athelstan (925-940). That monarch made a law forbidding the export of horses for sale, a circumstance which indicates that the horse trade with the Continent was even then considerable, and that ample use could be found at home for animals of good stamp. King Athelstan had probably interested himself in the improvement of the breed, for in his will, quoted by Berenger, he bequeaths the horses given him by Thurbrand, together with the *white* horses given him by Liefbrand. These donors were Saxons, so it is only reasonable to suppose that the animals they gave were representative samples of the Saxon breed, which was one of the Great Horse type.

FROM THE CONQUEST TO THE REIGN OF KING JOHN.

For six centuries after the Norman conquest the use of armour was universal. True mail of interlinked rings was generally adopted about the time of the Crusades (1190-94) and its use continued until the fourteenth century ; but from about 1300 the practice of protecting the more exposed parts of the body with plates of iron instead of chain mail began to extend, and the character of personal armour gradually changed until it became a complete panoply of plates. The

authorities give the period of mixed chain
and plate armour as from 1300 to 1410. By
the latter date this had disappeared in favour
of complete armour of plate, the use of which
continued until the beginning of the seventeenth century, growing heavier and stronger
in ratio with the increasing efficacy of offen-
sive weapons. We need not follow the
decadence of armour through the age when
buff coats and jerkins, under "demi-suits of
plate," were in vogue, to its final disappear-
ance far on in the seventeenth century. Our
concern lies with those ages during which
heavy armour was in use; for this was the
long period when the development of the
Great Horse was continuously the anxious
care of kings and parliaments. The steady
increase in the weight of armour is a factor
of the first importance in our present investigation; for therein we find the sufficient
motive which impelled our ancestors to
develop to the utmost the size and strength
of the only breed of horse which could carry
a man-at-arms. When we find that the
weight a horse might be called upon to bear
amounted to 4 cwt.—32 stone—at the period
when plate armour reached its maximum
strength, no further stress need be laid on
the power of the animal required. We

may find opportunity later on to consider in minuter detail the weight of armour.

At an early date we find the chroniclers speaking of the horse used in warfare as *Dextrarius* or *Magnus Equus ;* later on the English terms " War Horse " or " Great Horse " are used indifferently as the equivalents of the Latin. The history of the period between Henry II.'s accession (1154) until the reign of Elizabeth (1538-1603) shows that it was the constant aim of the Legislature to increase and improve the stock of these horses in England. In Henry II.'s reign several foreign horses were imported (A.D. 1160); but there is nothing to show to what breed these belonged. Maddox's *History of the Exchequer* contains mention of disbursements " for the subsistence of the King's horses that were lately brought from beyond the sea ; " but unfortunately we are not informed for what special purpose they were procured. It is more than probable that they were Norman horses suitable for breeding stock to carry men-at-arms ; for the first years of Henry's reign were spent in evolving order from the anarchy which England had endured under his predecessor Stephen—a task which implied forcible measures. The earliest

mention of " Cart Horses " that we have
found is made by one William Stephanides,
a Canterbury monk born in London, who
wrote in the year of Henry II.'s accession :—

" Without one of the London City gates is a certain
Smoothfield [Smithfield]. Every Friday there is a
brave sight of gallant horses to be sold. Many come
out of the city to buy or look on—to wit, earls, barons,
knights and citizens. There are to be found here
maneged, or War Horses (*Dextrarii*), of elegant shape,
full of fire and giving every proof of a generous and
noble temper; likewise Cart Horses, fit for the Dray,
or the Plough or the Chariot."

At this time, therefore, it appears that
horses were beginning to replace oxen to
some extent, and at all events for farm and
draught work ; but it would not be safe to
conclude that the animals " fit for the Dray
or the Plough or the Chariot " were of the
Great Horse stamp ; probably they more
nearly resembled the inferior animals which
were used for light cavalry purposes.

THE GREAT HORSE IN THE THIRTEENTH CENTURY.

Passing over the short reign of Richard,
we come to the time of King John (1199-
1216), a period of special importance in our
survey ; for we have definite particulars of
the importation into England during John's

reign of one hundred stallions of large stature from the low countries—Flanders, Holland and the banks of the Elbe; and it is from the blending of these sires with English mares in the lowland and shire countries that some strains at least of our modern heavy horses must be held to date their origin. Size and improvement were evidently not developed with the steadiness or rapidity desired by those who had the welfare of the country at heart; several Acts of Parliament were passed with this object in view.

We obtain an interesting glimpse of the comparative value of the Great and other horses at the end of the thirteenth century from records preserved in Bain's *Calendar of Documents relating to Scotland.* Among the Documents is a "Roll of the horses of banerets, knights, esquires, and vallets of the K.'s household [King Edward I.] valued in the Scottish war, 26th yere" [of the King's reign, *i.e.*, 1298]. This refers to a lengthy list of the horses which were killed at the battle of Falkirk, and from the items we quote the following :—

"Sir Thomas de Morham a black horse, 24 marks killed in the battle of Falkirk; Sir John Botetorte had a white pied charger value 60 marks

2

killed there; Guy Botetorte his brother had a black hackney value 8 marks killed there . . . Sir Henry de Beaumont had a brown bay charger worth 60 marks killed at Falkirk; Sir Eustace de la Hecche had a bay charger with a white hind foot value 100 marks killed."

Numerous "hackneys" figure in the roll; and whereas the maximum value claimed for a hackney, or hack as we should now call it, is 10 marks, the smallest sum set upon a lost charger or Great Horse is 60 marks.

FROM THE TIME OF EDWARD III. TO EDWARD IV.

Edward III. (1327-1377) added measures dealing with the matter to the Statute Book. This King also, as history records, spent very large sums on horses. We find him indebted to the Count of Hainault to the extent of 25,000 florins for horses; and Mr. Edward Burrows in his Introduction to Lord Ribblesdale's *The Queen's Buckhounds*, says :—

"In the long lists which occur in the Exchequer accounts of the wardrobe of numerous classes of horses belonging to the King—coursers, palfreys, trotters, hobbies, genets, hengests and somers—the 'dextrarii' or great horses received most attention. Provision was made for 102 of their housings out of 441 ells of canvas and 360 ells of cloth. The boundary between the great cavalry establishments was formed by the Trent, the division to the north of that river having its separate 'custos' under the Master of the Horse. The studs were distributed among the King's manors, such as Windsor, Guildford, Odiham, Woodstock and Waltham. The due proportion of expense necessary was borne by the sheriffs of the various counties. Special provision was made for a tunic of blue and a cape of white Brussels cloth as the attire of 'John Brocaz,' styled in these records 'Custos equorum regis,' or 'Gardein de nos *grands chevaux*.' "

The great cavalry department of Edward III., Mr. Burrows adds, appears to have been kept at its full war complement for about twenty years, until the power of France was supposed to have been finally broken at Poitiers. Sir John de Brocaz and his son Oliver were employed by the King to buy horses in Gascony before the campaign of Crecy.

Richard II. also gave proof of his anxiety to improve the breed of horses by passing laws on the subject.

The troublous times of the Wars of the Roses (1450-1471) were productive of injurious results. Horses of power and substance were, of course, required for all military purposes, and "Strong Horses" were seized whenever found and pressed into service by the contending parties. The owners of many of the best horses seem to have sent them out of the country to be sold beyond seas lest they should be thus confiscated. The fame of the *Equus Britannicus* had ere this period spread to the continent, where a ready market awaited it; Sir John Hawkewood in his *Travels* states that in the States of Northern Italy English horses were cherished and sought for breeding purposes. For the twenty-one years during which England was the scene of civil war it was worth no man's while to breed, much less attempt to improve, the Great Horse; thus much of the good which had been done was nullified.

THE LAWS OF HENRY VII.

Henry VII. was fully alive to the desirability of fostering the breed, and during his reign (1485-1509) more Acts were passed to this end. At this time, says Polydore Virgil, the English were wont to keep large herds of horses in pastures and common fields; and when the harvest was gathered in the cattle of different owners fed promiscuously together; for which reason the practice of cutting horses was introduced. The preference accorded horses for military use was not due entirely to their superiority in strength over mares; for centuries only entire horses were used by men-at-arms; this being the case the interests of discipline and good order in the ranks and at the horse pickets in camp practically compelled the exclusion of mares. In the eleventh year of his reign (1496) Henry VII. passed a law forbidding the export of horses. In the preamble it was set forth that whereas "not only a smaller number of good horses were left within the realm for the defence thereof, but also that great and good plenty of the same were in parts beyond the sea which in times past were wont to be within this land; whereby the price of horses is greatly increased here to the loss and annoyance of all the King's subjects;" therefore it was enacted that no horse at all was to be transported out of the kingdom, and no mare of the value of six shilling and eightpence or upwards. This law, it may be added, remained on the Statute Book until the reign of Charles II. when it was repealed. There were sundry weak points in the wording of this Act—in which respect legal draughtsmen will remind us it does not stand alone—and from the measures dealing with exportation which were passed by his successor it would seem that Henry VII.'s attempt to keep horses at home proved something of a failure.

To show what stage of development the Great Horse had reached in the time of Henry VII., art comes to our aid in the shape of a picture by Albert Dürer, dated 1505. This is the earliest work we have found, and though the animal portrayed is not of necessity an English bred Great Horse, it represents the stamp of animal then in use for similar purposes in Germany; and from the banks of the Elbe, as we have already seen, stallions were imported into England for the Royal Studs. It is quite possible that the horse whose portrait Dürer's brush has left us was one of English raising. A white horse of size, weight and power, such as this, was just the gift one ruling prince might have sent to another at a time when animals of that colour possessed the peculiar ceremonial value to which reference has been made, and it is far from unlikely that this particular animal was a royal gift from Henry VII. to Maximilian I. or to some other German prince. However that may be, two things are certain; it was a war horse, as the dress of the soldier attendant indicates; and the height, bulk, sloping quarters, abundant mane and tail, and well

1505

THE GREAT HORSE
after the Picture by Albert Dürer

feathered legs, prove it an example of a breed intimately allied to, if not identical with, the English Great Horse.

Our Frontispiece is reproduced from an engraving of a picture by Hans Burgkmair, a German artist, who lived 1473-1529. It not only affords an excellent idea of the stamp of horse ridden by armour-clad knights of the period, but also of the armour borne by the horse.

THE LAWS OF HENRY VIII.

In Henry VIII.'s reign (1509-1547) special attention was directed to the breeding of strong horses; new laws were made which sought to secure strength and stature by requiring sires and dams of a certain size and mould. Breeding was allowed only under restrictions, and a distinct element of compulsion is the enactment that all prelates and nobles ("whose wives wore French hoods or velvet bonnets") should maintain stallions of the required standard. The law passed in 1535 (26 Hy. VIII.) runs :—

" For that in many and most places of this Realm, commonly little Horses and Nags of small stature and value be suffered to depasture, and also to cover Mares and Felys of very small stature, by reason whereof the Breed of good and strong Horses of this

Realm is now lately diminished, altered, and decayed, and further is like to decay if speedy Remedy be not sooner provided in that Behalf."

" It is provided that all Owners or Fermers of parks and enclosed grounds of the extent of one mile in compass, shall keep two Mares, being not spayed, apt and able to bear foals of the altitude or height of thirteen handfuls at least, upon pain of 40/."

" A penalty of 40/ is imposed on the Lords, Owners, and Fermers of all parks and grounds enclosed as is above rehearsed, who shall willingly suffer any of the said Mares to be covered or kept with any Stoned Horse under the stature of fourteen handfuls."

The year 1541 saw another statute (32 Hy. VIII.) This enacted that—

" No person shall put in any forest, chase, moor, heath, common, or waste (where mares and fillies are used to be kept), any Stoned Horse above the age of two years, not being 15 hands high, within the SHIRES and territories of Norfolk, Suffolk, Cambridge, Buckingham, Huntingdon, Essex, Kent, South Hampshire, North Wiltshire, Oxford, Berkshire, Worcester, Gloucester, Somerset, South Wales, Bedford, Warwick, Northampton, Yorkshire, Cheshire, Staffordshire, Lancashire, Salop, Leicester, Hereford, and Lincoln."

" And furthermore be it enacted, that if in any of the said drifts, there shall be found, any mare, filly foal or gelding that then shall be thought not to be able nor like to grow to be able to bear foals of reasonable stature, or not able nor like to grow to be able to do profitable labours, by the discretions of the drivers aforesaid or of the more number of them, then the same driver or drivers shall cause the same unprofitable beasts, and every of them to be killed, and the bodies of them to be buried in the ground or otherwise bestowed, as no annoyance thereby shall come or grow to the people, there near inhabiting or thither resorting."

By another Act the exportation of horses beyond the seas is strictly forbidden ; and this Act is extended to Scotland ; selling a horse in England to a Scotchman without a Royal permission, is declared to be felony in both buyer and seller (32 of Henry VIII. cap. 6). This statute is entitled, "An acte for the tryall of felonies upon conveiynge of horses into Scotland."

The use of the word "Shire" will be noted in the foregoing extract. It is of interest in view of the diversity of opinion expressed when the Shire Hòrse Society was formed, concerning the propriety of using this term. In this statute of Henry VIII. for the first time we find the word "Shire" used in connection with horses

Ralph Holinshed, in his Chronicles (Ed. London, 1807, vol. vi., p. 3), has an entry which indicates that this monarch set his subjects a good example in this particular respect :—

King Henry VIII. erected a noble studderie for breeding horses, especially the greatest sorte, and for a time had verie good success with them. The officers however seemed wearie : and procured a mixed breed of baser races, whereby his good purpose came to little effect."

That horses of "the greatest sorte" were
absolutely essential at this time the immense
weight of iron worn by both rider and horse
proves to us. The engraving represents a
knight clad in a suit of tilting armour, which
is now to be seen in the Tower of London.
This armour was described in 1660 as
having belonged to Charles Brandon, Duke
of Suffolk, Henry VIII.'s brother-in-law.
The Tower officials give the weight as
follows :—Man's armour, 99lbs. 9oz. ; horse's
armour, 80lbs. 15oz. The mail would fit
only a big and powerful man (none other
could profitably wear it) whose weight must
have been at least 16 stone. Thus we
have :—

	Lbs.	oz.
Weight of rider	224	0
Rider's armour	99	9
,, spear	20	0
Horse's armour	80	15
Total ...	424	8

or 30 stone 4lbs. 8oz. As we must allow
for the knight's clothing and the horse's
gear, bridle, &c., the total weight would not
fall short of the four hundredweight mentioned by the old chronicler quoted on the
next pages as the burden the Great Horse
will " carrie commonlie."

EQUESTRIAN FIGURE IN TILTING ARMOUR; Sixteenth Century.

QUEEN ELIZABETH'S TIME.

Holinshed gives a valuable account of the heavy horses of Queen Elizabeth's time (1558-1603). From his record we gather that at this period the Great Horse was no longer reserved exclusively for military purposes, but was in general use for farm and draught work. Holinshed's reference to the transport required by the Queen's retinue when she made her frequent progresses through the kingdom is testimony to her inordinate love of pageantry and display. Coaches, according to Stowe, had been introduced into England by FitzAlan, Earl of Arundel, 1580 (though Queen Mary had had one built for herself in 1556), but this mode of conveyance does not appear to have commended itself to Queen Elizabeth. She was, as history tells us, an admirable horsewoman, and we know that she rode behind her Master of Horse when she went in state to St. Paul's. The following passage from Ralph Holinshed's Chronicle will be found in book ii., chapter i. of the folio edition printed in London, 1587 :—

" Our horses, moreover, are high, and, although not commonlie of such huge greatnesse as in other

places of the maine, yet, if you respect the easinesse
of their pase, it is hard to saie where their like are
to be had. Our cart or plough horses (for we use
them indifferently), are commonlie so strong that five
or six of them (at most), will draw three thousand
weight of the greatest tale with ease for a long
journeie—although it be not a load of common usage
—which consisted onlie of two thousand, or fiftie
foot of timber, fortie bushels of white salt, or six and
thirtie of baie, or five quarters of wheat—experience
dailie teacheth, and [as] I have elsewhere remem-
bered. Such as are kept for burden, will carie four
hundred weight commonlie, without any hurt or
hinderance. This furthermore is to be noted, that
our princes and nobilitie have their carriage commonlie made by carts; whereby it commeth to passe,
that when the queenes majestie dooth remove from
anie one place to another, there are vsuallie 400 care-
wares, which amount to the summe of 2,400 horses,
appointed out of the countries adioining, whereby
her cariage is conveied vnto the appointed place.
Hereby, also, the ancient vse of somers and sumpter
horsses is in a maner vtterlie relinquished; which
causes the traines of our princes in their progresses
to shew far lesse than those of the kings of other
nations."

The loads so respectfully described by
Holinshed do not at first sight appear to
indicate any very remarkable draught power
on the part of a team of five or six horses;
rather the contrary. In regard to this,
however, we must bear in mind that three
hundred years ago the roads were so bad
and rutty that an empty waggon would be
harder to draw in those days than a heavily
loaded wain on a modern road.

The accompanying portrait of Sir Walter
Hungerford, Knight, of Farley Castle,
Heytesbury, is engraved from a picture in
the possession of Sir R. Hungerford Pollen,
Bart., at Rodbourne, Malmesbury. Sir
Walter was the eldest son of Baron Hungerford, who was beheaded July 28th, 1541.
Upon the accession of Queen Mary, Walter
Hungerford obtained a reversal of the
attainder imposed on his father, and re-
covered the family estates ; but the peerage
was not revived. Sir Walter retired from
political life and court intrigue, and, choos-
ing for his motto, *Amicis Amicissimus*,
devoted himself entirely to country pursuits.
He became widely known for the excellence
of his stud ; and the picture here engraved
bears the following inscription, " Sir Walter
Hungerford, Knight, had in Queene Elizabeth's tyme, the Second of her Raine, for
foure yere together, a baye horse, a blacke
greyhounde, a lanerett.* This offer was for
foure yere together, to all Eynglande, not
above his betters, he that shoulde showe
the best horse for a man of armes, a greyhounde for a hare, a haucke for the reyver,
to wine III hundred poundes, that was a

---

* The falconer's term for the male Lanner—a small hawk.

hundery the poundes apese. Also he had
a gerfalcon for the herne in Her Majesty's
tyme, that he kept XVIII. yere ; and offered
the lyke to flye for a hundred pounde, and
were refused for all."

This offer of Sir Walter's gives us the
right to assume that the type here represented was the one acknowledged at the
date to be that most approved in the
English Great Horse ; whilst the special
function of that horse was, still, to carry
"a man of armes." It can be seen that—
though the hair, both of the mane and legs,
has been manipulated to suit the fashion—
the tail still shows the characteristic abundance. Sir Walter Hungerford's horse is
certainly of the type of Albert Dürer's Great
White Horse, though it shows more evidence
of spirit and high action.

Instructive particulars concerning the
horses of this period are to be found in a
curious little black letter volume, entitled,
*The Art of Ryding and Breaking Greate
Horses*, written by Thomas Blundeville of
Newton Flotman in Norfolk, and published
in 1566 ; a second edition of which, " newlie
corrected and amended of manie faults
escaped in the first printing" was issued in
1580 ; the latter including chapters on breed-

SIR WALTER HUNGERFORD, KNIGHT, OF FARLEY CASTLE, HEYTESBURY.

ing horses. We may quote from Blundeville's pages a few passages which throw
light upon our subject :—

"Some men have a breed of Great Horses, meete
for warre and to serve in the field. Others have
ambling horses of a meane stature for to journey and
travel by the waie. Some again have a race of swift
runners to run for wagers or to gallop the bucke.
But plane country men have a breed only for draftes
or burden."

From the foregoing it would appear that
the lesser breed of agricultural horses (stots
and affers) was still in existence, though
the extract on page 34 appears to show that
mares of the Great Horse breed were used
for draught purposes. It will be remem-
bered that at an earlier age churchmen were
enjoined to use mares that the horses might
be at the service of soldiers. Thomas
Blundeville mentions as the "most worthy"
breeds :—

"The Turke, the Barbarian, the Sardinian, Napolitan [commonly called the courser of Naples], the
Jennet of Spain, the Hungarian, the high Almaine,
the Frizeland horse, the Flanders horse, and the Irish
hobbie."

He describes these in turn: those that
come within our purview are the Napolitan,
high Almaine and Flanders: the first of
these is :—

"a trim horse being both comelie and stronglie made and of so much goodness, of so gentle a nature and so high a courage as anie horse is. Known from other horses by his no lesse cleane than stronge makinge."

The high Almaine (modern Allemagne, German : King John's importations from the banks of the Elbe at once recur to mind) is :

"commonlie a great horse, and though not finelie yet verie stronglie made and therefore more meete for the shocke [of battle] than to passe a cariere or to make a swift manege because they be verie grosse and heavie, yet by industrie they are made lighter behind than before, for their rider do use in their maneging to make them to turne alwaies with their hinder parts and not with their fore parts like jacka-napes on a chaine, whereby they keep their horses heads alwaies upon the enimie."

The Flanders horse differed little from the "high Almaine" or North German breed save that it was for the most part of greater stature ; the disposition of these two heavy horses was "not evill ;" on the contrary the animals are stated to be " verie tractable."

Thomas Blundeville's suggestions for breeding, based as they undoubtedly were on experience, throw light upon the ancestry of our heavy horses :—

" I would wish him that seeketh to have a race of good horses, meet to serve in the field to get a Napolitan stallion if it be possible, if not let him take the high Almaine, the Hungarian, the Flanders, or the Frizeland Horse, so that he be of convenient stature well proportioned and meete for the purpose. The mares should be of an high stature, stronglie made, large and fair, and have a trotting pace as the mares of Flanders and some of our own mares be. For it is not meete for divers respects that horses of service should amble."

The "Napolitan stallion," coming from a greater distance and being more costly, was comparatively seldom imported; whence the author's reservation "if it be possible." There is no doubt but that the English Great Horse owed far more to importations from more northern countries than to those from Italy.

A "horse of service," we are informed, should be able to

"trot cleane and loftilie, to stop lightlie, to turn on both hands readilie, to gallop stronglie, to manege with single turne surelie and last of all to passe a cariere [i.e., "do a smart spin"] swiftlie; and in all his doings from the beginning to the ending to reine well and to bear his head steddilie."

The "cariere" was to be of specified length; for a "mightie puissant horse great of stature" a shorter one was recommended.

In the chapter headed "How to ride a Horse to the best shewe before a Prince"— how to show him off to the best advantage, as we should say—there is a very suggestive remark which proves how necessary were the endeavours of horse-loving sovereigns to improve the breed :—

" Maneging and doubling after a cariere belongeth to a horse of greate force, which indeed should represent in his doings the verie order of fight observed in the field *which is but little used now a daies because of the general weaknes of our horses.*"

In the earlier edition the writer speaks with admiration of the Great Horse,

"not finelie yet stronglie made he is of great stature. The mares also be of a great stature ; strong, long, large, fayre and fruitful ; and besides that, will endure great labour in their wagons, in which I have seene two or three mares to go lightly away with such a burthen as is almost uncredible."

" But now to content the countryman his desire, which seeketh to breede horses for draught or burthen, where should I wysh him to provyde hymselfe of Mares and Stallions better than here in Englande."

" I have knowne some carriars that go with carts, to be so exquisit in their choyse of horses, as onlesse been as commely to the eye as good in their worke they would not buye them ; insomuch as I have seen somtyme drawing in their carts better proportioned horses than I have knowne to be fynely kept in stables, as jewels for the saddle. The horse that is meete for the cart, may serve also for the burthen, bycause he is strong and able to beare much."

In the second edition, however, we find the recommendation to the countryman to provide himself with stock of English raising qualified by a remark which confirms the author's reference to the general weakness

of the war horses of the time, and indicates
that the "misfits" of the Great Horse breed,
as we might suppose, were relegated to the
waggon and the plough. The passage "But
now to content. . . . . better than here in
Englande," continues :—

"whereas he maie easilie find a number of strong
jades more meet for that purpose than for the saddle,
and all for lack of good order of breeding which if it
might be once observed in this realme I believe there
would be so good and so faire horses bred here as
in anie place in Christendome."

The need of more legislation on the subject, or better administration of the existing
laws, is here very plainly indicated.

When discussing the advantages of gelding
horses for use on the road, Blundeville in-
cidentally bears out what we already know,
viz., that the animals used by heavily
armoured cavalry were entires. "Our light
horsemen here in England," he says, "do
in like manner serve upon geldings in the
warres . . . . partly for servants to ride
on and to carie their males [mail] and cloke
bagges."

The invention of gunpowder and its
application to hand firearms produced the
inevitable effect upon heavy armour in the
last quarter of the sixteenth century. Sir
John Smythe writing in 1589, the year after

the famous Spanish Armada fiasco, says
contemptuously of the cavalry of Spain :
" Their horsemen also serving on horseback
with launces or any other weapon they think
very well armed with some kind of head-
piece, a collar, and a deformed light bellied
beast." The introduction of coaches at
this time, and the encouragement of racing
at a somewhat later period also tended to
encourage the breeding of lighter horses in
England.

JAMES I.

We now take leave of our Elizabethan
instructors and come to records relating to
a generation later. In the Herbert MS.,
published as vol. xx. of the Montgomery-
shire collection, we find on page 148 an
estimate of the cost of horsing an expedition which was being fitted out to enforce
the claims of the Prince Palatine, son-in-law
to James I., to the Crown of Bohemia.
This estimate was laid before the Privy
Council on January 13th, 1620. Ten thousand
men were to be despatched from England ;
it was calculated that the baggage of this
army would weigh 1,150 tons, to transport
which as many carts each carrying one ton,
would be needed, and for each waggon eight

cart horses. It was further estimated that
for the conveyance of the officers, the sick
and the wounded, 380 waggons would be
wanted, and that three horses must be provided for each of these vehicles. The scheme
laid before the Privy Council proposed that
part, at least, of the 10,412 cart horses thus
required should be taken up where they
could be hired by the day " in the Low
Countries or where they may best be hadde.
They with the carters to drive and keep
them." The hire was estimated at 2s. per
diem, while the cost of the horses, if bought
outright, " with harness and furniture," would,
it was anticipated, be £9 apiece. The
framers of this estimate appended thereto
a note or recommendation which reflects the
comparative merits of English and foreign
cart horses at the time. " We think it necessary that, besides, 200 strong cart horses
such as cannot be hired should be bought or
continually kept for the use of the ordnance
and munition." The cost of these Strong or
Great Horses was put down at £15 per head
—the modern equivalent of that seemingly
modest sum being perhaps £100—and the
lieutenants and deputy-lieutenants of counties
throughout England were to be required to
certify what proportion of horses fit for this

service " each sheire canne affourd upon all occasions on enterprise."

Among the leaders of this expedition was the Duke of Arenberg, whose portrait, painted by Vandyke, is in the collection of the Earl of Leicester, at Holkham Hall, and from which the accompanying engraving is taken. In Smith's *Catalogue of Painters*, vol. iii., p. 148, this is described as one of the great artist's most successful equestrian portraits. Vandyke is believed to have visited this country in 1620 and to have executed commissions for James I. who conferred upon him a pension and a safe conduct which enabled him to travel without hindrance through all continental countries whose sovereigns were friendly to England. The picture affords interesting proof of the close resemblance of the English war horse in the first quarter of the seventeenth century to that portrayed by Albert Dürer more than one hundred years earlier. The colour is different; but in all material points it is practically identical with the white Great Horse of the German painter. The similarity of character is not confined to the horse on which the Duke is mounted; in the background a body of cavalry is represented, and an engraving on large scale of this portion of

THE DUKE OF ARENBURG; after the Picture by Vandyke.

the picture shows the stamp of animal to
be the same.

CHARLES I.

Coming now to the reign of Charles I.
(1625-1649) we find that the popularity of
racing and its results on the breed of strong
horses were disturbing the minds of thought-
ful men. Sir Edward Harwood presented
to the King a memorial which represented
that there was a great deficiency of good and
stout horses for the defence of the Kingdom,
insomuch that it was a question whether it
could have furnished 2,000 that would have
been equal to 2,000 French. The cause
being, the memorialist stated, the strong
proclivity of the nation for racing and hunting, which required horses to be lighter and
weaker for the sake of swiftness. Sir
Edward proposed as remedy that nobles and
gentlemen should keep stronger horses and
train them and their riders in military exer-
cises instead of making races for Bells. This
sound advice might have produced results
but it was offered at the time when troubles
were gathering about the throne and the
King had no leisure to attend to it. Charles
was fond of the *manège* and was a good

horseman ; his care for the art of riding the
Great Horse was shown by a proclamation
issued in the third year of his reign. In this
he commanded that, as he had found by
experience, such horses as are employed in
the service are "more apt and fit to be
managed by such as shall ride them, being
accustomed to the Bitt, than the Snaffle
. . . no person shall in riding use any
snaffles but Bitts only." This was qualified
by exception in favour of "times of Disport,"
which doubtless referred to racing, hunting,
and hawking.

It is quite in accord with King Charles'
love of the *manège* and military horsemanship
that the Great Horse should figure on the
Great Seals of the unfortunate King. By
permission of Mr. Allan Wyon we reproduce
from his beautiful work, *The Great Seals of
England*, engravings of Charles' Counter
Seal and Second Counter Seal with the
descriptions therein given. The engraver
has rendered the breed of his horses unmis-
takeable ; and nothing need be added to
Mr. Wyon's descriptions :—

COUNTERSEAL.
Period of use 1625 to 1627.

" The King on horseback, galloping to the left,
holding in the right hand a sword which passes
behind the King's head, the left hand holding the

COUNTER SEAL AND SECOND COUNTER SEAL OF CHARLES I.

reins. The helmet is ensigned with the Royal Crown. Three very long and three short feathers fly backwards from the King's helmet. The horse's neck is protected at the back by plates, and on its head is a plume of feathers. The horse wears a stiff caparison as in the seal of James I., but more limited in dimensions. On the caparison covering the hind quarter are the Royal arms encircled with an inscribed Garter, and ensigned with a Crown. In the lower border of the caparison thistles and roses are placed alternately at a small distance apart, above a short fringe. The reins are very wide and much ornamented; the part which is seen in front is escalloped, having four pendants, each pendant being made to represent a rose with a tassel hanging from it. The tail is in three distinct waves. In base is a greyhound collared and current to the left. The field is diapered with interlacing ovals, in which appear roses and thistles alternately. The legend begins with a rose, which is repeated between the words and is also placed after the last word. Between the first and last rose is a fleur-de-lis." Legend :—

CAROLUS . DEI . GRATIA . MAGNÆ . BRITANNIÆ . FRANCIÆ ET HIBERNIÆ . REX FIDEI . DEFENSOR, &c.

SECOND COUNTERSEAL.
PERIOD OF USE 1627 TO 1640.

"The King on horseback, galloping to the left, in complete armour, the helmet open showing the features very characteristically rendered, holding in the right hand a sword which passes above the helmet, and the point of which touches the outer border; the left hand holds the reins; on the left is a small shield covering the elbow and the lower part of the body. Two very large feathers sweep backwards from the helmet and two smaller ones rise to the outer border above. The right hand, the sword, and part of the helmet, break across the inner border and divide the commencement from the end of the legend. The horse is entirely devoid of armour. The saddle cloth is very small, and square. In base is a greyhound collared and current to the left, and underneath the horse is a view of London from the South, showing the river Thames and London Bridge. Shipping on the river below London Bridge is seen between the hind legs of the horse. The hills to the North of London are represented as of mountainous height. The hind hoof breaks into the legend."

CAROLUS . DEI . GRATIA . ANGLIÆ . SCOTIÆ . FRANCIÆ . ET . HIBERNIÆ . REX . FIDEI . DEFENSOR.

" The style of the King, which in the First Seal of his reign was ' Rex Magna Brittanniæ ' is now ' Rex Angliæ Scotiæ,' &c."

From the year 1200 downwards very many seals have borne the device of a horse, and invariably one of the Great Horse type.

FROM THE COMMONWEALTH TO WILLIAM III.'S TIME.

During the Commonwealth (1649-1659) three seals were in use, each of which shows on the reverse side a Great Horse of well defined character. To prove the use of the breed at this period we may, however, take evidence from Vandyke, whose equestrian portrait of Oliver Cromwell, in the heroic attitude orthodox for so many generations, is here reproduced. The charger upon which the Protector, partially clad in armour, is

THE PROTECTOR ON A GREAT HORSE; after the Picture by Vandyke.

represented, has all the Great Horse character. Stress must be laid on the fact that
from about this period the term Black Horse
is used as synonymous with Great Horse.
The following brief note from Cromwell
to Auditor Squire, which we take from
Carlyle's *Letters and Speeches of Oliver
Cromwell,* has value in this connection, as
also in showing the cost of troop horses at
the time :

" Stilton, Jan. 31, 1643.

" DEAR SIR,—

    " Buy those horses, but do not give more than
18 or 20 pieces each for them, that is enough for
Dragooners. I will give you 60 pieces for that Black
you won [in battle] at Horncastle, for my son has a
mind to him.

" Your friend,
"OLIVER CROMWELL."

It is altogether improbable that the "dragooners" referred to were animals boasting
the power and substance of the charger on
which Vandyke has painted the Protector.
Cromwell's "Ironsides" were not clad in
plate armour but in leathern jerkins, and
for men so accoutred a much lighter stamp
of horse would suffice.

In another letter written six months after,
appears the following phrase :—" I will give
you all that you ask for that black you won

last fight." Use of this term still survives
in a negative form among the breeders of
Cleveland Bays ; whose favourite boast of
their strain is that it contains " neither
blood nor black."

The actual value of the "piece" mentioned
is not quite certain. Mr. Warwick Wroth of
the British Museum (Department of Coins) to
whom I referred the point writes : " I think
that 'piece' must mean 'broad piece,' *i.e.*,
the gold sovereign (20s.) of the time called
'Unite,' 'Broad' or 'Carolus' (or if of
James I. the 'Laurel,' 'Jacobus,' &c.). The
only other coin that could be meant would
be the silver crown piece (5s.) of Charles I.,
or possibly the 'piece of eight,' *i.e.*, the
Spanish dollar current in England about
1643, for rather more than 4s." My in-
formant kindly sends me a quotation from
Rogers' History of Agriculture and Prices,
which confirms his cautious opinion that
the "piece" was the gold piece, *i.e.*, the
sovereign. The quotation referred to pos-
sesses an interest germane to the subject
under consideration apart from this special
point; it runs :—

" There is very little change in the price of horses
. . . during the first thirty years of my period [1582-
1702]. Then the price begins to rise for the next thirty

years and, though the dear decade 1643-1652 does not represent the highest average of the whole, the exaltation over the thirty years that precede it is very marked. For the period 1673-1682 horses are decidedly dear. Thus in 1673 a horse is bought by All Souls College at £30 5s., and two others at Cambridge at £20 each. In 1674 Winchester gives £15 8s. 6d. for a saddle horse."

Cromwell's letter was written at the beginning of the "dear decade;" and as the prices quoted for individual purchases thirty years later appear "decidedly dear" in a general review of the period, it is highly probable that £18 or £20 was the amount Cromwell thought "quite enough for dragooners." His offer of three times as much, £60, for "that Black you won" shows the superiority of the Great Horse.

Despite the prowess of Cromwell's lighter cavalry, the day of the true Great Horse was not yet at an end. In the year 1658 the Duke of Newcastle published his classic volume — *The Manner of Feeding, Dressing and Training of Horses for the Great Saddle and Fitting them for the Service of the Field in the Time of War*. This very curious and instructive volume, which was originally published in French at Antwerp contains numerous elaborate copper-plate engravings, most of which represent horses of the one massive type with large limbs, heavy

crest, silky haired fetlocks and flowing
mane and tail. The Duke writes of the
Northern Horses, using the term to dis-
tinguish the North German, Flanders and
similar breeds from the lighter Oriental and
Spanish horses :—" I have seen some,
beautiful in their kind, genteel in all sorts
of paces, and which have excelled all others
in leaping. Moreover they have a peculiar
excellence in the motion of their forelegs
which is the principal grace in the action of
a horse." Thomas Blundeville in his book
gives instructions for improving the action
of a horse ; he was to be taken into a
ploughed field or soft ground and en-
couraged with voice and spur to trot ; by
which exercise he would learn to lift his feet.

The engraving of a dappled grey horse
here given is from one of the latest works
of Paul Potter ; the original picture bears
date 1652, and was therefore painted only
six years before the Duke of Newcastle's
book appeared. Potter, who died at
Amsterdam in 1654, made his great reputa-
tion by the infinite pains he bestowed on
the study of cattle and sheep, and the success with which he gave the result of his
observations on canvas ; and it is only
reasonable to suppose that he exercised equal

A GREAT HORSE OF ABOUT 1652; after the Picture by Paul Potter.

care in painting horses. The strain of North German and Flanders blood was at this period so strongly represented in our English Great Horses of the best stamp that we need not enquire whether this horse was of German, Flemish or English origin ; the character of all being practically the same. The abundance of the plaited mane will be remarked in this picture.

The reflection that the Duke of Newcastle's careful work came somewhat late to fulfil its direct purpose crosses the mind of the student. During the latter half of the seventeenth century armour fell into disuse, and the interests of Great Horse breeding appear to have been neglected. Charles II. was a racing monarch, and James II. during his brief reign seems to have done nothing. William III. established a riding academy and brought over a French riding master, one Major Foubert, to direct it. The Great Horse, no longer required for military service, was no longer a saddle horse, and took its place as a beast of draught. From this time forward, therefore, we shall give it the name which associates it with agriculture and commerce, and speak of the SHIRE HORSE.

QUEEN ANNE'S REIGN.

In the reign of Queen Anne (1702-1713), the roads throughout England were still of the worst description, and the ponderous carriages of the nobility demanded great strength and weight in the animals which drew them ; and thus we now find the Shire Horse in demand as a carriage horse. The Queen's state coach was drawn by long-tailed Shire mares ; and the stage coaches which since 1670 had opened regular communication between London and the most important towns in the kingdom were we need not doubt, drawn by horses of a heavy, massive type ; for until the end of the century, when McAdam introduced the system of road making known by his name, no team of lighter horses would have been equal to the work. The value and importance of the Shire horse therefore in no wise decreased when the abolition of armour enabled our ancestors to employ a lighter stamp of cavalry trooper.

The *London Evening Post*, of September 24th to 27th, 1737, contains notice of a race which shows that endeavours were made to encourage the breeding of active cart horses. It runs as follows :—

" To be run for on Finchley Common, in the
county of Middlesex, on Tuesday the 4th of October
next, a Set of Lating Bells and Whip, for five Horses,
by Carthorses that constantly go in a Team, and to
be rid by the Carter that did constantly drive the
Team ; to ride bareback'd, with the Bit-Halter and
his own Cart-Whip ; to run two miles at a Heat, the
best of three Heats, and to pay three shillings
entrance, and no less than five to start, and enter the
day of running between the Hours of Eight and Two,
at the place above-mentioned ; the first Horse to have
the Bells, and the second the Whip."

Here is the advertisement of another race
of somewhat similar character which, in spite
of the element of jocularity in the conditions,
would help to stimulate the interest taken by
carters in their charges. This is taken from
the *London Evening Post*, of September 4th
to 6th, 1739 :—

" On the Wash, near Newbury, in Berkshire, on
Friday, the 22nd of September, 1739, will be run for,
a set of Cart Harness with Bells, for five Horses
(given by the Most Honourable the Marquess of
Carnarvon), by any Horse, Mare, or Gelding that
shall be 15 hands high at the least, and has been
train'd to the Cart only, and in that way continued
to be used. None but Carters to ride, and to ride
with Bell Halters, long Cart Whips, in Straw Boots
and Carter's Frocks, and without saddles ; and all
Riders to change their Horses, &c. (mares or geldings),
before starting at the Starting-Post, and no Man to
ride his own Horse (mare or gelding), &c., the Horse
(mare or gelding) &c., that comes in last to win the
Prize. And if any Dispute shall arise about the
Change of Horses, starting, running, &c., the same

4

to be determined by the said Marquis, his deputy, or deputies, and 2s. 6d. will be given by the said Marquiss to each Rider."

Marshall in his *Rural Economy of Norfolk*, published 1795, describes the road races in which "the lead was the goal contended for:" in his time this dangerous amusement, as he justly considered it, had been "a good deal laid aside though not entirely left off." The gist of Marshall's account has been given in a former little work.*

From *Heavy Horses* (No. 3 of Messrs. Vinton's Live Stock Handbooks Series), we take the following interesting passage which shows the value set upon good Shires, by their owners in the middle of the eighteenth century:

"Only within the last year or so there went over to the great majority . . . an old stud groom, whose grandfather in his day was at the head of a famous stud owned by people of the name of Gallemore, who for generations had a celebrated Shire stud within two miles of Calwich Abbey. At the time when Prince Charlie marched on Derby in the famous '45 this old retainer was forced to take refuge from the invaders and place the stallions of this stud in a place of safety. This he successfully did."

The fear lest these animals should be appropriated by the invader reminds us of

---

* *Harness Horses*. By Sir Walter Gilbey, Bart. Published by Vinton & Co., London.

the similar state of affairs three hundred
years previously, when the Wars of the
Roses created a demand for horses which
private owners took extreme measures to
avoid satisfying at their own expense
(pages 19-20).

This excerpt also furnishes us with a link
between past and present; for volume i. of
the Shire Horse Stud Book contains mention of several of the orginal Derbyshire
stallions named Gallemore, which were no
doubt called after their owners. The stud
referred to was stabled at Croxden Abbey—
"and from its courtyard the horses went
forth into hiding. Though it cannot be
stated as an absolute fact, all the evidence
points to the famous Packington Blind Horse
having been begotten at this same place"
(*Ibid.*, p. 16).

The direct descendants of the Packington
Blind Horse (believed to have been in his
full vigour from 1755 to 1770) are traced
down to the year 1832.

It is certain that this breed, for which
War Horse, Great Horse, Old English
Black Horse or Shire Horse are terms used
at different periods, has been distributed for
centuries through the district between the
Humber and the Cam, occupying the rich

fen lands of Lincolnshire and Cambridgeshire, and extending westward through the
counties of Huntingdon, Northampton,
Leicester, Nottingham, Derby, Norwich and
Stafford, on to the Severn. It has also been
extensively bred in the low-lying pasture
lands of England, in the counties both
north and south of those named, everywhere
retaining its typical character subject to
slight variations produced by differences of
climate, soil and food.

When Arthur Young, in the latter part of
the last century, was describing his tours
through the counties of England and Scotland, he mentions only two varieties of Cart
Horse as deserving attention, namely, the
Large Black Old English Horse, "the produce principally of the Shire counties in the
heart of England and the Sorrel-coloured
Suffolk Punch for which the sandy tract of
country near Woodbridge is famous."

The writer's use of the word " Shire " will
be remarked ; we cannot doubt but that a
breed of horses whose home was in these
counties would have been known in other
localities as " Shire Horses," like the " Norfolk Trotter" and " Suffolk Punch," and at
a later date the "Clydesdale ; " the only
difference being that the Shire was dis-

NORFOLK CART HORSE, DODMAN. Foaled 1780. After the Picture by Woodward.

tributed over a larger breeding area, which therefore furnished him with a less strictly local name. Arthur Young, it will also be observed, describes the breed as the " Large Black Old English Horse," a name which, as we have seen, had been in current use since at least the time of Oliver Cromwell. The Eastern counties breed was known and described as the Black Lincolnshire Horse. Black and grey, as Mr. Reynolds points out, were held to indicate purity of breeding.

We have now reached a period when painters of animal pictures were sometimes commissioned to execute portraits of fine examples of horses, cattle and sheep. The engraving which faces this page is from a picture by Mr. Woodward of a Norfolk Cart Horse called DODMAN (East Anglian for " Snail "), of whose pedigree unfortunately no particulars exist, but which was foaled in the year 1780. This horse was the property of an ancestor of Anthony Hamond, Esq., and the portrait is preserved at his family seat in the parish of Westacre near Brandon. The long hair-lock hanging from the knee arrests the eye ; this appendage, like a moustache on the upper lip and a hair lock projecting from the back of the hock, is regarded as the distinguishing mark of a

strain or variety of the Shire. DODMAN
seems to have been used as a stallion in
the district whence was obtained, nearly a
century later, HONEST TOM (1105), whose
portrait faces page 60.

Our next engraving is from a picture by
George Morland, which was probably painted
at about the same date as that of DODMAN.
That artist, between 1790 and 1795, went
into hiding in Leicestershire to escape from
his creditors; he took up his abode in the
neighbourhood of Mr. Bakewell's famous
Dishley Farm; and the horse portrayed
resembles in no small degree pictures of
some of Mr. Bakewell's stud, which at that
period had attained its highest repute. It is
therefore exceedingly likely that this represents a typical Leicestershire Cart Horse of
the time. It belongs to a type differing in
some respects from DODMAN, being longer
in the body, finer about the head and lacking
the hair-lock in front of the knee, while the
mane, tail, and feathering on the legs are less
profuse. These two portraits afford opportunity of comparing two varieties of the
Shire, the Fenland and the Leicestershire.

The *Sporting Magazine* of 1796 contains
an article headed "Operations on British

A LEICESTER SHIRE HORSE (1790–1795); after the Picture by George Morland.

Horses," in which the following passage
occurs : —

"We have a large and strong breed in the more
fertile and luxuriant parts of the island; and there is
no country can bring a parallel to the strength and
size of our horses destined for the draught, as there
are instances of single horses that are able to draw
the weight of three tons."

The roads in England had been vastly
improved since Holinshed described the
drawing powers of a team of horses in the
latter half of the sixteenth century; but we
cannot doubt that the horse itself had also
improved, more especially during the eighteenth century when the Great Horse was
gradually becoming the servant of the
farmer rather than that of the soldier. The
Statutes to which reference has been made
unquestionably did much to promote the
building up of the Great Horse breed and
establish it as national; the counties and
districts enumerated in 32 of Henry VIII.
quoted on p. 24 show very clearly how wide
was the area over which the breed was distributed three and a half centuries ago ; and
it would be superfluous to lay stress upon
the increase of the area over which the Shire
horse has been bred since that remote day.

It would seem that the action which our
forefathers sought to develop in the Great

Horse was still characteristic, in some degree
at least, of the Shire at the end of the last
century; this engraving, published at the time,
shows a horse named ELEPHANT, whose portrait was painted in 1792 by an artist whose
name is unknown. An inscription on the
frame tells us that this horse was "supposed
to be one of the most boney horses ever
seen;" at four years old he "is said to
have stood 16·2" and to have girthed 8 feet,
while he measured round the knee-joint $16\frac{1}{2}$
inches. He was plainly a horse of great
muscular development and big bone, while
his attitude suggests the activity and spirit
that distinguished the War Horse from
which he was descended.

From one of Garrard's pictures now hanging in the Council Room of the Shire Horse
Society, we take our engraving of this
gelding which was in use at Whitehead's
Brewery in 1792, and was therefore a con-
temporary of the horse painted by George
Morland, and of ELEPHANT. This picture
served as an illustration in Garrard's series
of engravings of British Farm Stock. It is
the likeness of an excellent horse—"type
perfect, flat bone, with good hocks, pasterns
and feet." Apparently this is a fen-bred
horse; a chestnut with the white face and

SHIRE HORSE, ELEPHANT (about 1792).

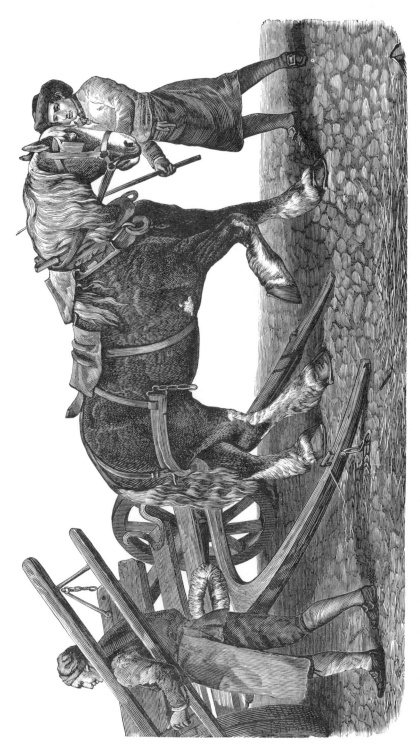

PORTRAIT OF A SHIRE GELDING IN USE AT MESSRS. WHITBREAD'S BREWERY IN 1792; after the Picture by Geo. Garrard, A.R.A.

markings which we have, of late years, learned to associate with the stock of the Rutlandshire Champions. High prices were paid for Shires in the last quarter of the eighteenth century. Mr. Hambleton of Callon Moor sold to Mr. Summerland in 1778 a brown stallion for 350 guineas; and in 1791 a two-year-old stallion named Marston was sold by Mr. Handley for 500 guineas; these would be good prices for pedigree stock at the present day.

It is worth adding to the portraits of Shire Horses foaled during the last decades of the eighteenth century one more showing a pair whose colour betrays them as belonging to a variety closely allied to that last noticed. The picture facing page 58 shows two horses named PIRATE and OUTLAW, and was painted in 1810 by an artist named J. C. Zeitter; the owner of the work was Mr. Andrew McCullum, and it was engraved by J. Egan.

These particulars we obtain from an inscription on the frame of the work, which is our only source of information. Having an eye to the accessories in the background, we infer that Pirate and Outlaw were, like Garrard's horse, the property of a brewer; both before and after this period views of

well-known breweries were favourite subjects
with some of our best animal painters, who
found excellent reason for their preference
in the magnificent teams of dray horses of
which private firms were so proud. The
ownership of, and work performed by, these
horses, are however of no special importance ;
the interest of the picture, apart from the
substance and strength of the animals, lies
in the colour. This curious parti-colour is
by no means uncommon in the Shires reared
in the Fen country ; in the middle of the
present century Mr. Colvin, of Pishobury,
Sawbridgeworth, Hertfordshire, had a breed
of Shire piebalds on his Home Farm. Mr.
Charles Marsters, of Saddlebow, King's
Lynn, Norfolk, possessed a celebrated
stallion, "England's Wonder," foaled in
1871 ; this horse was the sire of good
animals, but many of them horses of odd
colours. To this day there is a tendency
to breed animals with white legs, white
markings and odd colours.

THE SHIRE HORSE IN THE NINETEENTH
CENTURY.

It may be of interest to see how the east
country Shire appeared in the eyes of a very
competent judge of horseflesh about the time

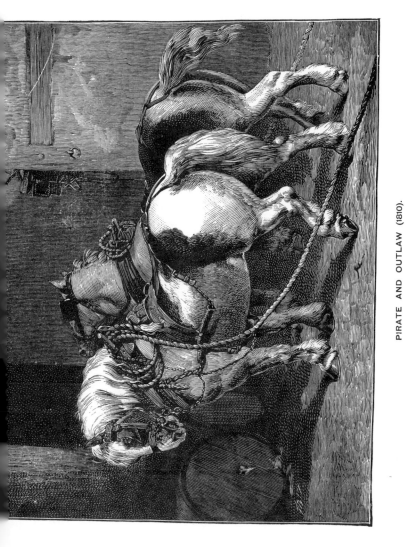

PIRATE AND OUTLAW (1810).

PLOUGH TEAMS OF SHIRE HORSES. Bred by B. B. Colvin, Esq., of Pishiobury Park, Harlow, Essex, about 1844-1855.
(Drawn by P. Palfrey, from a Photograph.)

of Waterloo. Thus the traveller George
Borrow, in his sketch of Tombland Fair,
Norwich, where from time immemorial a
show of stallions has been held at Easter :—

" There was shouting and whooping ; weighing and
braying ; there was galloping and trotting ; fellows
with high-lows and white stockings—and with many
a string dangling from the knees of their tight-breeches
—were running desperately ; holding horses by the
halter, and in some cases dragging them along.
There were long-tailed steeds and dock-tailed steeds
of every degree and breed. There were droves of
wild ponies, and long rows of sober Cart Horses.
There were donkeys and even mules ; the last a rare
thing to be seen in damp misty England ; for the
mule pines in mud and rain, and never thrives so
well as when there is a hot sun above and a burning
sand below. There were—oh, the gallant creatures !
I hear their neigh upon the winds ; there were—
goodliest sight of all—certain enormous quadrupeds,
only seen to perfection in our native isle ; led about
by dapper grooms ; their manes ribbanded and their
tails curiously clubbed and balled. Ha ! ha ! How
distinctly do they say, Ha ! ha ! "

When Borrow wrote this he had seen
specimens of pretty nearly all the draught
horses in Europe : including all the grand-
fathers of all the Percherons and Normandy
carriage-horses.

The old paintings and engravings, examples of which we have introduced as far
as possible in chronological order, possess
practical value to breeders as showing the

stamp and character of the Shire Horse at various periods of the history of the breed. We have traced its progress down to a date when the Stud Books relieve us of the necessity of further pursuit, and can only hope that success has attended this endeavour to show that our modern Shire Horse is descended from the animal which has filled so important a part at all times in the history of our country. It is also certain that during this century the Shire Horse has played no mean part in building up size and massiveness in all the other Draught breeds in the Kingdom. That he has undergone great changes is certain ; but the characteristics of the breed, size, strength, substance, courage and docility, have been perpetuated and developed by careful selection till we have now in our Shire horse the ideal beast of draught.

BLYTHWOOD CONQUEROR, whose portrait faces page 64, stands as an excellent representative of the modern Shire stallion. This horse is by Hitchin Conqueror (4458) out of Blythwood Bountiful (11607), and was bred at Wood House Farm, Stansted, by Sir James Blyth. He was foaled in 1893, and is a bay, with white blaze and white feet.

HONEST TOM 1105.

17½ Hands.   Foaled 1865.   By Thumper 2123, out of Beauty.   Bred by Mr. W. Welcher, Watton, Norfolk.

HOW TO PRESERVE ITS CHARACTER.

To maintain the standard of excellence which has been attained at the cost of so much care, it is essential that only the best types should be used for breeding : such horses as are truly framed, are free from imperfections, and above all are free from hereditary unsoundness. The numerous statutes mentioned in the foregoing pages assisted our ancestors in building up the breed which has long been established as permanent. The longer a type has been *fixed* the greater the certainty that the law " like produces like " will be justified ; and to secure the best results it is of the first importance that we should study the pedigrees of the animals from which we propose to breed.

The sight of the magnificent teams which may be seen in the streets of our great cities, and under particularly favourable circumstances on Whit Mondays at the Cart Horse Parade in Regent's Park, proves what careful and *continued* attention to the science of breeding can produce in the way of attaining desired results in size and form. For many years past there has been a regular and extensive demand for massive horses of

great muscular strength ; bad roads made
such animals indispensable up to a hundred
years ago : and the heavy loads which our
level streets and highways permit render the
same qualities not less necessary now. To
drag heavily laden waggons and drays, to
shunt railway carriages and trucks, we need
horses of the Shire stamp and character at
their highest development ; for it must be
borne in mind that a compact, truly framed
draught horse will move a given weight
with far greater despatch and less chance
of injury to himself than one whose shoul-
ders are defective, whose loins are weak,
legs ill formed, pasterns too long and feet
defective.

THE FOREIGN MARKET.

It is noteworthy as proof of our dependence
on this class of horse that, even when commerce and agriculture have been passing
through a period of depression, at times when
customers at any price even for the best
classes of other live stock have been difficult
to find, heavy draught horses suitable for
town work have always remained in brisk
demand at remunerative prices. Within the
last few decades, too, new and important
markets have been opened in all parts of

the world. The United States of America took many of our best Shire horses every year until the introduction of prohibitive import tariffs ; these naturally administered a severe check to the trade ; but there is good reason to believe that the present year (1898) has witnessed a revival. Our best European customers now are the Germans ; and of more remote buyers, the breeders of the Argentine Republic. It must be stated, in connection with what has been said on a previous page concerning the importance of studying pedigrees, that foreign buyers, though ready to pay large sums for our best, will possess themselves of the best only. Their object is to perpetuate the Shire breed pure, and also to improve the bone, size and substance of native breeds ; and with this purpose in view they are invariably most exacting on the points of pedigree and soundness. They know that good pedigree and soundness are essential, and require that their purchases shall not only be registered in the Stud Book, but shall be able to show the clearest record of descent ; such record shows that the qualities of the individual horse are hereditary, and may be relied on as transmissible to its progeny.

Important testimony to the value of the

Shire Horse will be found in a report issued some few years ago by the Canadian Government. It includes portion of a letter from Mr. R. S. Reynolds, M.R.C.V.S., Veterinary Inspector to the Corporation of Liverpool, and a well-known judge of and writer on Draught Horses. Mr. Reynolds, after writing fully on draught horses generally, concludes his remarks as follows :—" My judgment is entirely in favour of the Shire, as the one best calculated to procreate a breed—suited for the purposes of heavy draught—from smaller and lighter mares." He assigns as his reason the fact that the size and bone of the average Shire are superior to those of any other description of horse ; and further because there is presumptive evidence that the increased frame and bone of the other draught breeds are due to the infusion of Shire horse blood. Mr. Reynolds also strongly asserts his belief that, the original type of every other draught breed being of much lighter build than the existing race, there will be marked tendency in the progeny of such breeds to revert to the original form. Not only when these interbreed will this tendency appear, but when crossed with mares of other blood deficient in bone, degeneration will be still more rapid.

BLYTHWOOD CONQUEROR.

Many old paintings and mezzotint engravings exist to show us the type of Great or Shire Horse as it was bred at various epochs of our history, more or less remote. Some of these have been deposited at the offices of the Shire Horse Society ; and these likenesses, often the work of the first painters and engravers of their day, suffice to show that in massiveness and general character the heavy horses of England were much like those of to-day. We have now many horses whose pedigrees are traced in the first volume of the Shire Horse Stud Book for at least a century and a half ; back to a date which was within a lifetime of the last days of armoured knights carried by Great Horses. It is this long line of descent which guarantees the continued transmission of valuable qualities.

The paintings and engravings, as also the written accounts of the breeds of draught horses in the United Kingdom up to the middle of this century, depict them as of medium size, and it is only by the blending of the "Shire" with the blood of such stock, that they rival the latter in massiveness.

THE SHIRE HORSE SOCIETY.

It is impossible to close this slight review of the history of the breed without reference

5

to the very important services which have
been rendered by the Shire Horse Society.
This Society originated in the work of a
few men who desired to make an organised
endeavour to improve and promote the
breeding of the English cart horse by dis-
tributing sound and healthy sires throughout the country. Public attention was first
drawn to the matter in the year 1877,
when Mr. Frederic Street read his paper on
" The Shire Horse " at the Farmers' Club.

The Society was founded in 1878 as the
" English Cart Horse Society," it became in
1884 the " Shire Horse Society": and under
the latter name has continued to confer on
tenant farmers the benefits which accrued
from the date of its establishment. The
work of the Society and the eagerness with
which breeders have availed themselves of
its labours may be seen from the nineteen
volumes of its Stud Book. The first volume
is a monument of painstaking research ; it
contains the pedigrees of upwards of 2,380
stallions, many of which were foaled in the
last century. These invaluable records were
supplied by members from almost every
county in England ; and their compilation
was a task to which Mr. R. S. Reynolds
devoted years. The second volume was

published the year after the first, and the Stud Book has since been published annually. The nineteenth volume issued at the beginning of the present year shows the total number of animals registered to be 42,304, viz., 17,101 stallions and 25,203 mares.

The entries during the current year are, I am informed, not far behind the large total of 1897; this is the more gratifying in view of the fact that more stringent conditions of registration have been imposed. It is not desired to overload these pages with statistics; but the following few figures quoted from the Report of the Council in March last will serve to show the progress made in the last fourteen years.

	1884	1898
Number of Members	903	2237
Entries in Stud Book for year ...	1423	3581
Value of Prizes given	£524	£1200

The last eleven volumes of the Stud Book have contained in each year tabulated lists of prizes won; thus displaying fully a very important appendage to a pedigree. The illustrations, some from paintings, others from photographs of stallions and mares which have taken the Championship at the Society's Annual Show, which are to be found in each volume, possess not only an instructive value for the breeders of the day, but as time goes on will form a series of the utmost interest and importance as the pictorial record of the progress of the breed. The essays on breeding and management which are to be found in these volumes, coming from experts who are not only masters of their respective subjects, but who possess the gift of lucidly conveying their knowledge, enhance the value of the Stud Books in no small degree.

The Show held each spring serves a double purpose in promoting the interests of the breed and keeping breeders in personal touch with one another to the advantage of all. It may be worth giving here, in condensed form, the number of entries received for the Shows of the last ten years since the first edition of this little book was published.

		1889	1890	1891	1892	1893
Stallions	...	276	480	332	337	294
Mares	...	171	166	165	224	213
Geldings	...	—	—	—	—	—
		447	646	497	561	507

		1894	1895	1896	1897	1898
Stallions	...	268	241	263	319	300
Mares	...	207	226	223	217	210
Geldings	...	—	22	17	17	16
		475	489	503	553	526

Many causes operate to produce fluctuation in the numbers of entries; but the general average is well maintained, and the quality of exhibits, as the auctioneers' returns prove, continues steadily to advance.

The Society has numbered among its Presidents His Royal Highness the Prince of Wales, who takes a keen personal interest in the breed above all others associated with agriculture, and has owned a stud for many years; the Earl of Ellesmere; Earl Spencer, K.G.; the Hon. Edward Coke; the Earl of Powis; the Duke of Westminster, K.G.; Mr. William Wells of Holme Wood, Peterborough; Lord Egerton of Tatton; Mr. Anthony Hammond of Westacre, Norfolk; Lord Wantage; Mr. Chandos-Pole-Gell; Lord Hothfield; Mr. R. W. Sutton Nelthorpe; Lord Belper; Mr. A. C. Duncombe; Lord Tredegar; and Mr. A. B. Freeman Mitford.

For myself I may say in all sincerity that the year 1883, when I had the honour of holding office as President of the Society, and the year 1897 when again I was paid the compliment of being asked to fill the Presidential chair will always remain in memory as among the pleasantest in a tolerably active life.

SHIRE HORSE SOCIETY

The position in 1975

In the lean years which followed the war, few people ever thought that the Shire Horse would come back into its own as it has in the last five years. Today the Society is thriving with nearly 1,500 members, who are enrolling at well over 100 each year.

Over 100 horses have been exported to America, Canada, South Africa, Sweden and Switzerland. More and more horses are being used in commerce and on the land, and many more people are setting up studs.

Prices for horses both in this Country and abroad reached an all time high, with foals fetching between £500 and £1,500. Fillies and mares between £500 and £2,000 and colts fetching as much as £4,000. These figures were unheard of in the late 1960's. Entries in the Stud Book have doubled.

A Stallion Premium Scheme was set up in 1972 through a generous increase in the Grant from the Horserace Betting Levy Board. The Society now has a *Shire Horse of the Year Championship* at the Horse of the Year Show at Wembley, generously sponsored by J. R. Parkington & Co. Ltd., the New Bond Street Wine Merchants. Southern British Road Services Ltd., have entered into a collective sponsorship at six Shows in the Southern counties. Shires at many other Shows are now being sponsored and today, when the judging takes place the Shire Horse ring is always one of the centres of attraction.

The newly opened Courage Shire Horse Centre at Maidenhead Thicket opened in April, 1975, attracted 80,000 visitors in its first year—more than many of our stately homes.

The Shire Horse Society is administered from the offices of the East of England Agricultural Society, East of England Showground, Peterborough, and the Secretary is Roy W. Bird, who would be very pleased to enrol new members and to supply information on the Society and Shire horses in general.